Beat The Crash Volume 1

Truth About ETF Rotation
-
Fund Your Retirement by Investing in Top Exchange Traded Funds in One Hour Per Week

By Jackie Ann Patterson

©2012-2013 Own Mountain Trading Company

Published by:
Own Mountain Trading Company dba BackTesting Report
P.O. Box 620427
Woodside, CA 94062-0427
+1 650 752 4921
support@backtestingreport.com
www.backtestingreport.com

Despite best efforts to produce a useful and correct report, this book may contain errors. Much of the data relies on backtesting, which is a historical simulation with significant differences from real live investing and trading. No claim is being made that you will make money from this book, and in fact you may lose money from investing. The author is not a licensed financial planner. You must consider carefully what is right for you and consult professionals as needed.
This book is intended for educational purposes and is not a recommendation to buy or sell securities.
HYPOTHETICAL OR SIMULATED PERFORMANCE RESULTS HAVE CERTAIN LIMITATIONS. UNLIKE AN ACTUAL PERFORMANCE RECORD, SIMULATED RESULTS DO NOT REPRESENT ACTUAL TRADING. ALSO, SINCE THE TRADES HAVE NOT BEEN EXECUTED, THE RESULTS MAY HAVE UNDER-OR-OVER COMPENSATED FOR THE IMPACT, IF ANY, OF CERTAIN MARKET FACTORS, SUCH AS LACK OF LIQUIDITY. SIMULATED TRADING PROGRAMS IN GENERAL ARE ALSO SUBJECT TO THE FACT THAT THEY ARE DESIGNED WITH THE BENEFIT OF HINDSIGHT. NO REPRESENTATION IS BEING MADE THAT ANY ACCOUNT WILL OR IS LIKELY TO ACHIEVE PROFIT OR LOSSES SIMILAR TO THOSE SHOWN.

For my mother,
who set an example
of kindness and generosity.

Contents

Introduction....5

My Story...9

How to Compare Investment Strategies.....14

How Index-Makers Rule.....24

How to Create a Diversified Portfolio.....27

Performance of Buy-and-Hold of Diversified Portfolios.....37

What Could Be Better Than Diversified Buy-and-Hold.....53

How to Do an ETF Rotation.....54

Performance of Rotation of Reference Portfolio.....56

What If You Don't Own a Home?.....63

Which Day of the Week to Rotate?.....66

Bring on the Long Bonds.....68

Shorting the Market with Inverse Funds.....70

How About Those Commodities?.....72

Everything But the Kitchen Sink.....73

Rotating to Cash when Everything Rots.....74

What Happened with Stop Losses.....78

Does Active Rebalancing Help Grab Profits?.....81

Double-Checking the Asset Mix.....82

Which Strategies Beat the Crash.....83

Resources.....88

Acknowledgements.....90

Introduction

You can retire in comfort and security. Your investments can provide for your living expenses and free you to live the good life. It is not that hard, but it will require you to master a few techniques to monitor the markets, keep your mind alert, and maintain the personal discipline to act decisively on occasion. Even if your life savings was devastated by the last decade, this book can give you the tools to help re-build it and get your retirement back on track.

As I write this, the world economy has been on life-support for years. Stimulus programs are a regular and familiar crutch. Interest rates wallow at all-time lows. The real estate market took a tumble and loans are not so readily available to fund a cash-flow empire based on rental property. Looking back over the last decade in the stock market, we've experienced tremendous gains and harrowing downdrafts. The only group that has done exceedingly well is bond investors, and that may well be escalating into the next big bubble.

Are the days gone when individuals like you and I could hope to support ourselves without depleting an account's principal in the process? Admittedly, it looks bleak. But what if you could sense when to approach the stock market aggressively and when to shift to a more conservative stance?

This is exactly what large money managers are doing with what they call "risk-on / risk-off" strategies. The idea is that when they perceive conditions are favorable to taking risk, they jump in the market full-force. As conditions shift to take on a dangerous tone, the risk-off orders go out, and the markets drop as the money takes flight to safety.

The trouble is that these money managers don't alert us, the general public, to their risk assessments. Instead they quietly pull out, selling the assets they believe are on the brink of disaster to an unwary public. After all, someone needs to hold the bag.

If you'd rather not be one of their stooges who buys at the top of the market only to learn about the big players getting out or even selling short, then the *Beat the Crash*™ series of books is for you. My goal is to lay out a set of data and indicators that you can reference to make your own call on when and how to participate in the market. Use the tools described in the pages that follow to help understand when it's a prime time to be in the market, and when a more conservative asset allocation is more likely to be rewarded.

The indicators and techniques chosen for the *Beat the Crash* series run the gamut from fundamental to technical to sentiment. Their common attributes are:
- Robust track record
- Apply to the broad market or economy as a whole
- Objective
- Relatively simple

This first book in the *Beat The Crash* series serves two purposes. As the title *"Truth About ETF Rotation"* suggests, the main idea is to show you how to put together a strategy that rotates among top Exchange Traded Funds (ETFs).

Before diving into ETF Rotation, this first book in the *Beat the Crash* series defines the standards we will use to evaluate whether an indicator or method can help us understand the market. It establishes a baseline for comparison – a reference point to see how well the strategies are working. To do that, we will look at simple ways to manage a diversified portfolio and decide where to invest funds when the game is on.

Clearly, I'm not advocating a buy-and-hold strategy, nor is it high-frequency trading either. Buy-and-hold leaves us vulnerable to large losses that take years to recover. In practice, it's a rare individual who actually carries out buy-and-hold. Instead, many people who set out to buy-and-hold lose their resolve after a market plunge, only to find they've sold at, or near, the bottom. Or, they make my friend's favorite mistake: buy a promising stock and hold through stellar gains, but end up selling for a small loss once it comes back to earth.

Just because we're not married to a stock or market outlook does not mean that we need to spend our days and dollars trading in and out frequently. That style of trading presents many challenges, both technical and psychological. It is increasingly dominated by automated high-frequency trading taking place in computer centers co-located with the stock exchanges.

Individuals have limited resources to compete in the high frequency trading game. Besides, I have no inclination to spend my retirement years staring at a computer screen! I'd wholeheartedly recommend that you balance your life beyond the markets as well. Remember, money management is a means to an end, not the end to itself.

If your end goal is indeed a better retirement, you may find you do better to practice these strategies in a retirement account. A self-directed IRA at a discount broker will do just fine. If your funds are stuck in a 401k with limited choices, you may have to adapt some strategies to the mutual funds provided and consider the 401k's restrictions on trading carefully before each move.

If, instead, you are investing in a regular brokerage account, you may be liable for taxes when moving money between asset classes. But even paying taxes is better than all-out losing your savings!

These strategies are meant to protect your nest egg as much as grow it. They attempt to point out the best times to risk money in the stock market and take defensive action when the going gets tough. No doubt we will sometimes experience losses even using the tools set out in the *Beat the Crash* series of books. We have only the assurance that we've done our best to learn from history rather than blindly repeat it.

The companion website for the *Beat the Crash* series of books is **beathecrash.com**. For this book in particular, you'll find the companion site at **truthaboutetfrotation.com**. See the Resources section at the end of the book for instructions on how to access the bonus materials including an ETF rotation forward-testing spreadsheet and trade-by-trade backtesting data.

My Story

Let me tell you my story. I am not a natural born investor or trader. Rarely graced with the intuition to do the right thing at the right time, almost everything I learned came through one of two ways: a series of hard knocks or exhaustive computer simulations. Even once I saw that money could be made in the stock market, I stumbled forward in the dark until certain events forced me to shed a little light on what I was doing. My purpose in writing this book is to help illuminate your path to greater success in the markets.

The truth is that I didn't set out to forge a career backtesting the stock market. In fact, I didn't even set out to trade the market. I am a computer engineer by training. What with stock options and living in Silicon Valley for the tech bubble in the late 1990's I couldn't help but notice that money came from the stock market.

I started out very conservative, figuring that I had very little so I better not lose it. I selected the most conservative choice for my 401k funds. Some so-called Guaranteed Fund, something about investment-grade insurance blah-blah-blah -- I didn't look that closely but "Guaranteed" sounded good.

Ha! The Executive Life insurance industry debacle taught me that even the most conservative-sounding choices can blow up. It is important to understand what really underlies the marketing names. All was not lost though. Eventually money trickled out of the bankruptcy settlement. A few years ago I received a back payment from the Guaranteed Fund. Nice, but it's much less useful to be made whole 20 years later!

Working at a software company as the internet took off, I traded just for kicks. It seemed all my colleagues had their own little formula. The Altera rep to Cisco bought more stock in both companies each time he received a sales bonus, which was often. A marketing manager bought shares of whatever electronic company would try out his leading edge design product and he profited. I tried my hand at finding dot.com initial placements (IPOs) and flipping them as they caught on fire.

But I didn't make as much as I could. Being anxious that dot.com mania was too good to be true, I tried to make a more conservative allocation of funds. That's how I came to have my account balance once again slashed by holding a bond fund in a rising interest rate environment. I got around to fixing that just before the tech wreck induced a flight to safety of treasury bonds. I was yet to see that the choice of conservative versus aggressive allocation had more to do with the market state than my age, risk tolerance, and goals.

Like most adult Americans, I know exactly what I was doing on September 11, 2001. On a business trip to Boston, I had a little time in my room before my first meeting and was selling stock on my laptop. I'm not kidding, I was trying to place a sell order and NASDAQ was not responding. The room service waiter told me a plane had hit the WTC. My sell order was lost among the unfolding drama on television and my week-long adventure traveling home after Boston's Logan airport closed. When the markets re-opened several days later, I opened the brokerage window on my laptop once again. Not selling but buying. Not because I knew anything about bottoms or volatility or sentiment extremes but because I thought it patriotic to support the market with whatever I could muster.

Meanwhile, after more than a dozen years in industry the work felt like drudgery punctuated by corporate battles. I started to take financial independence more seriously. I'd learned early on not to trust financial advisors. I've lost enough being "put in" funds– thank you. I hate being "put in" funds. I decided to make time to seriously learn to manage my own money.

When I sold my house in Saratoga, CA in late 2002, I had more ready cash, and thought, "Now I can really give trading a whirl!" With what now, in hindsight, seems like amazingly little research, I plunked the proceeds of the sale into a couple stocks. Right there in the office, I just casually put my life savings on the line and went off to a meeting.

Right. I was quietly freaking out. Back in my office glued to my screen, I watched as every little tick of the stock prices drove my account balance wild. When it was up, visions of private jets flew before my eyes. When it was down, my whole insides just shriveled in fear – I couldn't even see straight.

Sometimes fear is the appropriate emotion. That was just too big, too reckless and I am too anxious to be doing that. I liquidated to cash, ran out of my office, and went for a blazing walk around the park thinking, "I'm sure glad I don't have to do THAT for a living!"

So back I came to "make a difference" in the corporate world with renewed vigor. My career enthusiasm didn't last long. Surviving something scary can be exhilarating and soon I was back looking for more exciting market adventures. Besides I wasn't so sure my current middle management position was really making much difference in the world anyway. On top of that my father had passed and I needed more time to help my elderly mother who came to live near me.

So I took classes, read dozens of books, and put together a trading plan that promised to set me free. I worked at it until I had a quarter where my profits matched my "day job". Then I set out on my own.

Ah the good life! I rafted the Grand Canyon, snorkeled Hawaii, took a trading class in Cyprus, another in Florida, and a third in Arizona. Every day, my laptop came out and I managed my trades before going back to my fun. I competed in the Spike Group trading contest, earning two silver medals for quarterly performance and growing confident.

Things started to change – gradually at first. Gradually as in that scene from the movie Jaws where the lady is treading water and first experiences a surprising little tug on her leg. Okay, that's too dramatic. You can see where I get anxious.

Really what happened is more subtle. While traveling in Europe, trading the US market is an after-dinner activity. One night, I got on the wrong side of a trade and couldn't let it go. Unfortunately, I stubbornly tried to tell the market what to do -- an expensive tantrum.

Next day, I thought it prudent to eat a little extra from the breakfast buffet and enjoy a light, inexpensive dinner. By Portugal, I was packing away boiled eggs from the breakfast buffet because that was going to be dinner as my trading losses grew.

No job and losing money in the market. How frightening is that?

I'd like to think I have other prospects. But I hear a younger woman sits in my office now. My secret fantasy working at REI with all the cool outdoor products doesn't include sore feet and embarrassment of waiting on my former colleagues. Anyway, the credit crisis and subsequent retail contraction took care of that.

No choice but to make money from the markets! Except that's way too much pressure to trade. With more computer skills than market savvy, I decided to sell my backtesting research to fund my ongoing studies of the market. Now I offer reports, videos, software and an alerts service to the public. Also, I do consulting on strategies for trading and investment.

The really great thing about starting this business turns out NOT to be the money. First off, it rekindled my love of computers, software and even customer support. But the best thing is really the amazing things I've learned from my clients.

One of my biggest clients, Fidelity Investments, asked me to write an article on sector rotation. I saw the potential of trading a rotation strategy but needed to work out a few issues raised in the article.

Well, "working out a few issues" amounted to developing my own portfolio simulation software, acquiring historical data, running endless tests -- basically starting over from scratch to research ETF rotation in the context of diversified portfolio management. This book is the summary of my new research.

To wrap up this story and get on with it, let me just say that the backtesting is paying off, I'm still independent, still traveling, still skiing, and a customer of REI instead of a job applicant.

One other important comment: I'm not a registered investment advisor. The quantitative results and discussion in this report are meant for educational purposes only – not specific investment advice. You are in charge of determining what fits your needs and temperament. All trading and investment comes with risk of loss and is not for everyone.

How to Compare Investment Strategies

This section discusses metrics to compare investment and trading strategies. Yes, it is dry, but the reading will make it easier to understand the nuances of the backtesting performance of the various strategies presented later in the *Beat The Crash* series of books. You may want to skip to the next chapter, **How Index-Makers Rule,** if you are already familiar with mathematic concepts or simply uninterested in delving deeply into investment return measurements.

Everything Is Relative

Is 6% per year a good return? It depends on your perspective. To investors looking to meet specific personal goals, such as providing for the kids' college or paying the monthly bills in retirement, the absolute return may be all that counts. If it meets the need, fine. If not, keep looking.

Relative returns, on the other hand, make a comparison to a benchmark because everything's relative. In a good year, a 6% return may seem quiet beside the roar of the market. In a crash however, it's a smug investor who comes out ahead by 6%.

What is the Golden Standard for Comparison?

The investment world tends to compare returns to one of two different standards.

The first is the risk-free return, typically assumed to be the interest paid by short-term US Treasury bills. This is often used in the risk / reward computations such as Sharpe Ratio, which is how it's used in this book.

Another tactic is to compare returns to the most relevant benchmark. For example, a stock mutual fund generally compares to the Standard & Poor's S&P 500® index and a bond mutual fund compares to a bond index.

The trouble is that both of these golden standards have been off their game in the last decade. Interest rates dropped through the floor, tempting conservative investors to take more risk to get anything back on their money. Since 2000, the secular bear market shredded the previously glowing stock market returns.

A Better Baseline

When deciding on an investment strategy, it's better to make relative comparisons between different strategies over the same time period. However, just comparing to non-existent interest rates or an erratic bear market is too easy.

A better baseline is one that produced decent returns and is also easy to operate. For the *Beat The Crash* series of books, a diversified portfolio of assets represented by mutual funds or Exchange Traded Funds (ETFs) will form the baseline. More on that in the upcoming chapter, **How to Create a Diversified Portfolio.**

What Metrics to Compare?

Having decided on a baseline for comparison, next comes the choice of what attributes of each investment strategy to compare. Read on for an overview of the metrics that will be reported for the baseline diversified portfolio and for each investment strategy in the *Beat The Crash* series of books.

Price Gains alone do not include dividend / interest payments so they do not present the whole picture even though they are relatively easy to come by. Typically, only price gains are presented in other publications. That is inaccurate and gives stocks an apparent advantage over bonds and other dividend-paying instruments.

Total Return is the price of the assets plus its dividend payments. Dividends do matter, especially when dealing with bond funds. This is also the money that ends up in your account! *Beat The Crash* will rely on total returns including dividends for both backtesting and reporting.

Returns may be expressed in several different ways, each with its own advantages and disadvantages.

Year-by-Year Return gives a feel for how the strategy performed. It exposes the trade-offs between strategies that may have similar average returns and varying volatilities. For example, this is where you can most simply see the difference between a strategy that plods along earning about the same per year versus a wild ride that wins big, loses big and averages out about the same. It is hard to compare lots of strategies year-by-year so this level of detail will only be presented in select situations.

Compound Annual Growth Rate (CAGR) is comparable to interest rates. Applying CAGR each year takes you from the initial account balance to the ending balance albeit more smoothly than the real ride. Geometric Mean is the general concept behind CAGR. The geometric mean is the metric of choice for academics interested in the Optimal Growth Strategy. Intuitively, it makes sense to make this as large as possible. Who doesn't want a fast growing portfolio, if all else is equal?

Average Return is easy to calculate as the arithmetic mean each period's return, but simply taking a starting account balance and applying the average return each year won't give the ending balance like CAGR. Keep in mind that a loss of 50% requires 100% gain to recoup!

Average return is also the mathematical expectancy, if the sample size is large. The arithmetic mean, along with variance, is the metric used by Modern Portfolio Theory, which forms the basis of your financial advisors' mandate to divide assets between stocks and bonds according to your age and risk preferences.

Excess Return Over "Risk-Free" Return shows how the strategy did compared to keeping the money in the safest known investment vehicle. The risk-free rate has varied considerably over the test period for these financial strategies. Many computations boil down the risk-free rate to one number to represent the whole test period. Instead, I use the actual rate of 3-month US Treasuries available on each day during the test period. I don't care if my stock holdings beat the average of risk-free rates, but I want to know if the stock strategies beat the risk-free rate offered at that time. This is especially important at the present time when the 3-month rate approaches zero but was up over 8% in 1990.

Risk Metrics

Imagining the upside of investment strategies is great fun but anyone who has ever put money in the stock market knows that it's not all beauty and grace. As prudent investors, we need ways to estimate how much the various strategies expose us to risk and how well they reward us for bearing risks.

Drawdown measures equity drops from peak to trough without regard to monthly or annual boundaries. It takes the high point of an account balance and subtracts the low point to tell you how much went missing during a market downturn. Once again, we will rely on total returns because dividends can soften the blow of drawdowns.

While drawdown is relatively easy to visualize, it is harder to plug into the probabilistic functions that allow us to compare risk-adjusted returns across different horizons and anticipate what else might go wrong based on what has historically gone wrong.

Volatility expressed as the **standard deviation** of returns is often adopted as a measure of risk because it is a way to quantify the possibility of nasty surprises. Computing the standard deviation allows the math geeks among us to use probability theory tools to estimate the likelihood of returns within a range.

Beware that the stock market does not follow all the assumptions that go with the usual probability estimates such as a normal distribution. Historically, the stock market has misbehaved much more often than would be expected according to probability theory. It is said that market returns exhibit "fat tails" because the occurrence of the unlikely hasn't dropped to nothing as quickly as the math might indicate.

Since most of us don't think in terms of probability distributions, the **Sharpe Ratio** is useful as a single metric that quantifies risk and return. It is defined as the average returns above a benchmark divided by the volatility or standard deviation of the returns above the benchmark. It can be calculated on either a monthly or annual basis.

A key decision when calculating the Sharpe ratio is what to use for the benchmark return. For simplicity, and since the annual returns are a broad brushstroke, a single number of 2.8% is used. That is the average annualized 3-month Treasury rate for the period of 1990 – 2011. When calculating the monthly Sharpe ratio, however, we're getting down into the gritty details and then the actual month-by-month 3-month Treasury rate is used.

Unfortunately, most documents and prospectuses do not disclose the benchmark used for the calculation of the Sharpe ratio. Also the Sharpe ratio will vary depending on the time period applied. For those reasons, it's actually dangerous to compare Sharpe ratios across various publications. Within the *Beat the Crash* series of books, you can be assured that the Sharpe ratio calculations are applied consistently and thus useful for evaluating the relative performance of the investment strategies tested.

As typically calculated, the professional measures of risk-adjusted performance carry us away from the notion that drawdown is the bad guy. Anything based on standard deviation as a measure of volatility penalizes us for upside gains as well as downside losses which may seem harsh. The common-sense explanation is that if something went up abruptly in good times it has the potential to go down sharply when things turn sour. Also, preference is given to strategies with more consistent returns rather than a few big winners because a consistently growing account balance makes financial planning easier.

Many other risk metrics exist. For example, the Sortino ratio is very similar to the Sharpe ratio except that it does not penalize for good returns because is based on the semi-variance. To calculate it, only the negative variance from the risk-free return was calculated. The Sortino ratio generally comes out with a larger number than the Sharpe ratio.

The *Beat the Crash* series of books will primarily report maximum percentage drawdowns, standard deviation, and Sharpe ratio to answer the key question: Did hopping in and out of the market actually improve the risk-adjusted performance for investors?

Other Interesting Statistics

Other statistics can be of interest when mulling over strategies. Highlights are

- Number of trades per year
- Average holding time of each trade
- Win rate (% of times selling for a profit)

Timeframes

Repeatedly, I've said that you can only compare certain metrics within the same time period. So what timeframes are we considering for these experiments in investment management?

The limiting factor is getting good data for the backtesting. US Treasury interest rate data back to 1990 is at our fingertips on the web. However, most of the interesting ETFs weren't available until 2005. Mutual funds pre-dated ETFs, however, passively managed mutual funds that follow market indices did not come into vogue until the 1990's. Yes, Vanguard came out with a fund that mirrored the S&P 500 in the late 1980's but it wasn't until 1997 that an interesting selection of index funds for foreign and domestic markets came out. On top of that, we need about a year's data to look back upon when making the first investment decisions in our strategies.

After careful consideration of all the factors, the simulation for this report will focus primarily on the following time periods:
- 2005 – 2011 for recent ETF performance
- 1998 – 2011 the largest period with enough funds to make ETF rotation interesting

Strategy Simulation via BackTesting

Backtesting measures the relative performance of a set of investment strategies by simulating the strategies on historical price data. Backtesting can be done by hand but is usually automated by computer software these days. The rules for buying and selling are objectively defined and programmed into the backtesting engine which proceeds day by day through the price data and records the results from all the trades.

Since backtesting relies on past data, it makes no guarantees about upcoming performance and can't say whether a strategy will do as well in the future as it did in the past. However, if a strategy didn't perform in the past, there's no reason to believe it will suddenly turn into a winner. It pays to avoid strategies with a losing track record.

Although most traders agree that backtesting is useful, many people don't do it because of the time, expense, and expertise required. To produce the relatively simple backtesting reports in this book, I spent nearly $1000 on data and two months part-time developing and testing the strategies.

Backtesting is not perfect. Although I've made the extra effort to include dividends which are typically not considered by commercially available backtesting engines, I did not model the effects of commissions or slippage. This matters more if you trade frequently or trade extremely large size.

Since most tactics in this book result in rather limited account activity, commissions probably do not play a huge role in the performance of the strategies in this book. In fact, at the time of this writing Fidelity Investments is offering commission-free trades on most iShares ETFs which are the instruments of choice to implement this rotation strategy. So the effects of commissions should be insignificant.

Other inaccuracies that may affect the results include my tactic of simulating the execution of buy/sell orders each day at the close, and assuming we get the closing price. Strictly speaking, this is peeking because we really can't know the closing value until it is too late to trade.

In practice, however, many of us check for trading signals at 3:30pm eastern time and squeeze in an order just before the close. Another approach for end-of-day trading is to set a limit order for the next day's open based on the closing price on the day of the signal. This can be a leisurely way to avoid slippage – until the market moves quickly and the trader is forced to play catch up.

Backtesting is not reality. It is a model of reality – like a flight simulator. I expect professional pilots to gain experience in a flight simulator, even though all the nuances of aviation are not modeled exactly. Just because a pilot does well in the simulator, it's no guarantee that he/she won't make an error in the air. But I really do not want to ride with a pilot that persistently crashes the flight simulator!

So it is with backtesting. It can tell us strategies to avoid – that's for sure. A strategy that passes backtesting qualifies for further investigation and controlled forward-testing before a prudent investor puts much capital behind it. And even then, it's wise to expect the completely unexpected and size accordingly.

How Index-Makers Rule

Since making relative comparisons is the way to assess market strategies, the first thing to do is establish a baseline for comparison. In the case of absolute returns, the baseline becomes the "risk-free" interest rate. Unfortunately, that rate approaches zero at the moment. For those interested in beating the market, some form of market return is needed for the baseline.

Academics and experts are quick to point out that the odds of doing better than average in the markets are slim. Just ask anybody that makes their living running index funds that invest in the averages.

Way back in time, the Dow Jones 30 Industrial Average seemed to be the favored market proxy. With the rise of index funds, the S&P 500 index of large company stocks became the poster-child for the stock market. I recall getting advice in the 1990's to simply invest in a fund that passively mimicked the behavior of the S&P 500 and call it good. People piled onto the indexing bandwagon and it seemed to work well. New funds sprouted that follow every conceivable index.

After the millennial market crash, the S&P 500 index was slow to get off the mats. Other areas of the market did better, notably small company stocks. The Russell 2000 index is the well-known benchmark for that segment.

Benefits of Following an Index

A key benefit of index funds is that they are diversified across many companies in their designated market segment. The Russell 2000 spreads the risk of small company ownership between 2000 firms. If any one of them hits the skids – which happens, especially early in the fight to establish a market base – the impact on the overall index is limited.

If a company should implode altogether, it is removed from the index and replaced with a stronger contender. Not immediately, though. If the company is still able to limp along it may be given a chance to correct its deficiencies. Also, some index-makers only realign according to a set schedule. Others re-jigger as it suits them.

Thus the indices enjoy an upwards boost from survivorship. The index shouldn't drop to zero unless whole segments of the market collapse. That obviously doesn't mean that a stock index can't make a severe drawdown, it just means that it is extremely unlikely to go out of business entirely.

Another advantage of index funds is that you don't spend time stock-picking. Maybe even more important to some people, is not second-guessing themselves over stock picks.

At the Mercy of the Index-Makers

What helps indices, and the companies in them, is that they are so widely followed. Individual companies benefit from inclusion in an index because everyone investing with index funds brings a higher level of sponsorship to the companies that comprise the index. This is no secret.

For example, on August 29, 2012, Sears was removed from the S&P 500 because it was deemed that its public float was not up to snuff. LYB was chosen as the replacement with no reason given. The news was announced before the market opened and at the open SHLD was down 4% while LYB jumped the same amount. The next day, SHLD, left to fend for itself, dropped 0.13%. LYB immediately got in line with its new brethren and closed up 0.47% compared to SPY 0.44% gain on the day.

Tracking the two days surrounding one index change does not constitute a comprehensive study. I just bring it up to illustrate the point. Apparently the market makers believed 4% was the value of being included in the S&P 500 index. 4%! No wonder few active fund managers can beat the index!

The not-so-good news is that we still haven't gotten away from people picking stocks. There is no God-given list of companies that make up each index. Instead there are sets of rules and committees of people that pick the companies that go in or out.

The proponents of index funds made a great case that people have difficulty picking stocks that go up. Unfortunately, that case applies to the index too! Warren Buffet once remarked that when the tide goes out, we get to see who is swimming naked.

The implicit stock-picking methods of the index-makers look good now, while index-following is favored by institutional and individual investors alike. Should indices fall from favor, the story may be different.

For now, it seems reasonable to follow the herd following the indices. Just stay alert to scandals that may cause a stampede away from indexing.

How to Create a Diversified Portfolio

This chapter defines a basic diversified buy-and-hold portfolio. Because the portfolio may turn out to be the bedrock of your investment strategy, the basic steps for creating and maintaining a diversified portfolio are laid out.

Why Use a Diversified Portfolio as a Reference for Comparison

The difficulty with using any one index as the baseline for comparison is that sometimes it represented the market well, other times not. In other words, sometimes it was the place to be, other times not.

Those who know we don't know in advance which asset class will do well often hedge their bets by diversifying their portfolio across many asset classes. Stocks, bonds, and real estate are the three primary choices. Of course, commodities, convertibles, and venture capital can be added to the mix, particularly for high net worth individuals. Index funds now make that easy for anyone to dabble in all the categories.

The two main advantages of using a diversified portfolio as our baseline for comparison are that it sets a high standard to beat and enables us to learn more about the basic skill of portfolio management. Also, by choosing a reference portfolio of index funds, we can make a direct comparison between the static buy-and-hold approach and strategies for rotation among the asset classes.

Altering the composition of the portfolio becomes the basis for risk-on / risk-off. Risk-on is achieved by adding more of the asset types deemed as risky-but-rewarding during situations where we have reason to believe taking on the risk will pay off more than usual. Risk-off is achieved by reducing the risky assets and emphasizing the asset classes believed to carry less market risk.

"Risk-on / risk-off" connotes extremes of being completely in or completely out of the market. While that is sometimes the case, it is perhaps more often advantageous to hedge our bets because:

- Markets have a random component and really anything could happen.
- Signals are mixed and murky most of the time.
- Distinct markets may be relatively uncorrelated much of the time, e.g. stocks and bonds.

A hard-core risk-on / risk-off which yanks funds completely out of the market became fashionable after repeatedly finding that in market crashes everything plummets together. For example, commodities and stocks may move independently much of the time. However, once the margin calls kick in during a crash, commodities and stocks race each other to the bottom. Later volumes in the *Beat the Crash* series of books will explore indicators to detect when to get completely out of the market.

What Asset Classes to Include in the Model Portfolio

Studies[1] show that the choice of asset classes can make a big difference in returns down the road. History records how various asset classes performed in the past and that's one factor to consider. Knowing that PAST PERFORMANCE DOES NOT GUARANTEE FUTURE RESULTS, let's tune in to our individual goals to help with the decision.

My goals for this book are to create a basic model portfolio that everyone can understand and use for comparison purposes.

If you're at a place financially where you are reading investment books, you probably have a good-sized nest egg to invest, and you probably own real estate. Any financial advisor would also tell you that you need a cash account for emergencies. Therefore, I am keeping those out of the model portfolio, even though I think it's a good idea to hold some cash and real estate, and in fact I do both.

My personal situation is that I've got a fair amount of gold tucked away in a bank vault – a legacy from dark days following a perma-bear advisor. So, as with real estate, I don't have the need to represent commodities in my portfolio. (Yes, I agree it would be better to have a diversified set of commodities but I'm not there yet.)

Your goals will be different than mine. Consider your situation carefully when deciding on your own portfolio. For more background information on portfolio management, see my reading list at backtestingblog.com/order/books.

The assets I chose for a well-rounded Model Portfolio are:
- US Large-Cap Stocks
- US Small-Cap Stocks
- International Developed Markets Stocks
- International Emerging Markets Stocks
- US Bonds

---

[1] Ibbotson, Roger G. "The Importance of Asset Allocation", Financial Analysts Journal, March/April 2010, Vol. 66, No. 2: 18-20.

Tactics for Implementing a Diversified Portfolio

To implement the portfolio, we have the following choices:

- Hold individual stocks, bonds, real estate in a mix that corresponds to the recommended split between domestic and international markets.
- Rely on a fund manager to pick individual instruments that represent each asset class.
- Rely on indices that track the stock, bond, and real estate markets. This choice can be implemented with either
  - o Mutual funds
  - o Exchange Traded Funds (ETFs)
- Recognize that owning a house and maintaining a reserve account for its upkeep probably more than satisfies the requirements for real estate and cash in the portfolio. Then only the stock and bond portions need to be represented by mutual funds or ETFs.

For the purpose of backtesting, it makes sense to use mutual funds to capture the most history and ETFs to model what an active investor might actually use. However, for your actual portfolio, you might want to consider the trade-offs.

The advantages of index funds – whether they are ETFs or mutual funds – was outlined in the previous chapter, **How Index-Makers Rule**.

The advantage of owning individual stocks is that if you hone your stock-picking techniques, you might wind up with winners that out-perform the indices and carry your portfolio to greater glory with less tax liability. On the other hand, picking dogs or hanging onto to winners until they turn into dogs can cost you. In fact, individual companies can disappear entirely, leaving stockholders with nothing but a tax write-off.

The advantage of owning individual bonds is that you can just hold onto them, receiving dividends until maturity when you get the principal back. Compare to bond funds where the price of the fund changes in response to interest rates. Yes, the market value of the bond changes over time too but you can just ignore it if you're intent on holding until maturity. The down side shows if you pick a bond that defaults on its obligations: doesn't pay its interest, doesn't return its principal. Bond funds make it easier to diversify against defaults.

Matching Funds to Asset Classes

For the backtesting reference portfolio, here's a list of funds which represent the chosen asset classes.

Asset	Mutual Fund	ETF
US Large Cap Stocks	VFINX	SPY or IVV
US Small Cap Stocks	NAESX	IWM
Int'l Developed Markets	VGTSX	EFA
Int'l Emerging Markets	VEIEX	EEM
US Bonds	VBMFX	AGG

Figure 1 – Asset Classes and Tickers

For US large-cap stocks, the S&P 500 is the undisputed choice. SPY, which tracks the S&P 500, is typically the ETF with the highest volume. No one is offering to let you trade that one for free! IVV is an ETF from iShares that tracks the S&P 500, which trades commission-free at Fidelity Investments (at the time of this writing). When implementing the US Large-Cap stocks with mutual funds, I chose VFINX – the Vanguard fund that started it all.

For US small-cap stocks, three different indices represent the space. The Russell 2000 is probably the most popular as IWM ranks among the top ETFs by volume. S&P also keeps the S&P Small-Cap 600® index. For mutual funds, again Vanguard has the longest history of small-cap indexing with NAESX, which tracks the MSCI US Small-Cap 1750.

For International Developed Markets Stocks, the EFA exchange traded fund tracks the MSCI EAFE® index. Right now, the Fidelity fund FSIIX passively tracks that same index. Unfortunately, no international fund on exactly that index has quite enough history for backtesting. The closest match is VGTSX which does allow us to backtest from 1998 but actually follows the MSCI All Country World ex-USA Investable Market Index. The upshot is that the model portfolio emphasizes emerging markets a little more in mutual funds than it does in ETFs.

International Emerging Markets Stocks are tracked by the ETF from iShares with ticker EEM and the Vanguard fund VEIEX, which both follow the MSCI Emerging Markets index. Note that with these index funds, we can invest in markets worldwide without taking the time to become familiar with their languages and stock exchanges.

US Bonds are represented by the Barclays U.S. Aggregate Bond Index, which is tracked by the iShares AGG exchange traded fund. VBMFX is the Vanguard fund counterpart. This bond index has a duration of 5-10 years which makes it less speculative than long bonds and more lively than short-term notes. It also features a mix of corporate and treasury bonds.

What Percentage to Invest in Each Asset Class

Now that we've decided on our asset classes, the next question is how much to invest in each.

Professional portfolios managers allocate their assets by computing percentages according to their model of risk/reward. The Nobel-Prize winning Modern Portfolio Theory (MPT)[2] takes advantage of the lack of correlation among diversified assets to create an optimal portfolio in terms of expected return for a given risk. Or, for a given risk tolerance, MPT can help find the portfolio weighting that produces the highest expected return.

As an aside, MPT relies on values for volatility, correlation, beta, and even expected return that are typically derived from historical price data. It is possible to plug in truly forward-looking expected returns, say by calculating a price as discounted cash flow of the underlying company but almost everyone looks in the rearview mirror for volatility and correlation.

Further complicating matters, professional suggestions for individuals' portfolios include a notion of investment horizon. They generally recommend putting more coin in stocks when one is young and directing a greater proportion of dollars to bonds in later years when one favors stability and income.

One rule of thumb is that the percentage of your portfolio in bonds should equal your age. Stock index fund proponents call that conservative though[3].

Detailing the models is beyond the scope of this report but keep in mind these methods result in dynamic portfolio allocations that change with the past performance of the market and the current needs of the investor.

---

[2] Markowitz, Harry. "Portfolio Selection", *The Journal of Finance*, Vol. 7, No. 1 (Mar., 1952), pp. 77-91. Published by: Wiley-Blackwell for the American Finance Association http://www.jstor.org/stable/2975974

[3] http://www.kiplinger.com/columns/fundwatch/archive/a-twofund-portfolio.html

Of course, many popular money guides give a simplistic one-size-fits-all investment allocation. For the purpose of a reference portfolio, I will calculate the returns on a several data points and use the middle one as the baseline going forward.

Setting up the Reference Portfolio

Getting started is easy. Finding the number of shares to buy for each element of the portfolio is a simple calculation. On the start date, for each fund, just multiply the account balance by the percentage allocated to the fund, and then divide by the current price of the fund. Round down to get the number of shares to buy.

For backtesting, I took the closing price on the start date. For real execution with ETFs or mutual funds, you may not be able to get that closing price due to slippage.

Slippage is the difference between the last quoted price and the actual price paid. With mutual funds, there is no slippage because everyone gets the same price – the Net Asset Value (NAV) at the close of trading. However, if you place an order after the market closes for the day, it will be filled at the next day's close of business, which is probably a different price.

Since ETFs trade like stocks, they have a price spread between the bid price and the asking price. If your quantity is large, you might absorb all the shares at the bid/ask and actually move the market with your order. That is slippage.

Limit orders can help slippage because they specify a set price for the transaction. In practice with thinly traded instruments, a limit order often means waiting until the market slips far enough past the set price that the market maker can scalp a profit by accepting your order. In some cases, the market may not come back to your limit price, leaving you to jump in with more slippage than if you'd just entered at the market price.

In markets with wide spreads and gentle movements, or very fast markets, you will probably find slippage unavoidable. I did not model slippage or commissions in the backtesting.

Rebalancing to Maintain the Portfolio

My earlier backtests on portfolios -- published in Fidelity Viewpoints and presented at MoneyShow San Francisco 2012 -- did not include rebalancing. It was only after contemplating the need for rebalancing in an ETF rotation strategy that I came to understand the benefits of rebalancing and actually implemented them in my backtesting tools. Now all my portfolio simulations include rebalancing.

Rebalancing is the cheat for buy-and-hold strategy advocates, allowing them to participate in more market action than simply allocating funds one time and letting her run. It is necessary because the more successful assets will come to dominate the portfolio over time which wrecks the diversification. The reason I call it a "cheat" is that it allows the buy-and-hold investor to take profits from assets that are up and buy into lesser performers, like a value investor might do.

Performance of Buy-and-Hold of Diversified Portfolios

Figure 2 below brings together the performance metrics for diversified portfolios with various stock/bond balances from a historical simulation of mutual funds held and rebalanced from 1998 – 2011.

The top line lists the stock/bond breakdown. For example, 70 / 30 means 70% stocks and 30% bonds. The stock allocation is split equally for each of our previous four categories of US large-cap, US small cap, developed markets and emerging markets. In our example, the 70% allocation to stocks is split with 17.5% of the total account going to each stock fund.

The portfolio simulator purchased the mutual funds in this proportion on the start date and then rebalanced on the first trading day in January of each subsequent year.

Comprehensive metrics are reported in the table. A more detailed description of the metrics is in the chapter **How to Compare Investment Strategies.**

1998 - 2011 Buy and Hold Portfolio Simulation with Mutual Funds
Funds: VFINX, NAESX, VEFX, VGTSX, VBMFX

Stock % / Bond %	90 / 10	80 / 20	70 / 30	60 / 40	50 / 50	40 / 60	30 / 70	20 / 80	10 / 90	SP500
Individual Stock Fund %	22.5%	20%	17.5%	15%	12.5%	10%	7.5%	5%	2.5%	VFINX
Net Profit on $10k init bal	$ 14,159	$ 14,693	$ 15,039	$ 15,211	$ 15,191	$ 14,941	$ 14,454	$ 13,861	$ 13,089	$ 6,340
Overall Profit %	142%	147%	150%	152%	152%	149%	145%	139%	131%	63%
CAGR %	6.5%	6.7%	6.8%	6.8%	6.8%	6.7%	6.6%	6.4%	6.2%	3.6%
Max DD %	-54.2%	-49.0%	-43.4%	-37.4%	-31.0%	-24.4%	-17.6%	-12.4%	-7.7%	-55.1%
Rough: Profit % / Max DD %	2.6	3.0	3.5	4.1	4.9	6.1	8.2	11.1	17.0	1.2
Max DD Date	9-Mar-09	9-Mar-09	9-Mar-09	9-Mar-09	9-Mar-09	9-Mar-09	9-Mar-09	27-Oct-08	29-Oct-08	9-Mar-09
Avg Annual Return	8.7%	8.4%	8.0%	7.7%	7.4%	7.1%	6.8%	6.5%	6.2%	5.5%
Annual Standard Deviation	21.0%	18.5%	15.9%	13.4%	10.9%	8.5%	6.1%	3.9%	2.3%	18.9%
Annual Sharpe Ratio (2.8% risk-free rate)	0.28	0.30	0.33	0.37	0.42	0.51	0.65	0.94	1.44	0.14
Avg Monthly Return	0.65%	0.64%	0.62%	0.61%	0.59%	0.57%	0.55%	0.53%	0.50%	0.41%
Monthly Standard Deviation	5.0%	4.4%	3.8%	3.3%	2.7%	2.2%	1.7%	1.3%	1.0%	4.8%
Avg Excess Monthly Return over 3-month Treasury Rate	0.43%	0.42%	0.40%	0.38%	0.37%	0.35%	0.33%	0.30%	0.26%	0.18%
Monthly Excess Standard Devia	5.0%	4.4%	3.8%	3.3%	2.7%	2.2%	1.7%	1.3%	1.0%	4.8%
Monthly Excess Sharpe Ratio	0.09	0.09	0.10	0.12	0.13	0.16	0.19	0.23	0.27	0.04
Monthly Excess Sortino Ratio	0.14	0.15	0.17	0.19	0.22	0.26	0.31	0.40	0.49	0.06
Total Trades	68	67	67	65	63	67	64	67	60	1
Win Rate	91%	93%	94%	97%	97%	97%	100%	99%	100%	100%
Lose Rate	9%	7%	6%	3%	3%	3%	0%	1%	0%	0%
Avg Win %	79%	82%	79%	91%	87%	87%	92%	81%	84%	64%
Avg Loss %	-8%	-8%	-7%	-10%	-10%	-10%	0%	-5%	0%	0%
Avg Bars Held	1820	1799	1821	1827	1757	1874	1843	1690	1606	3522

Hypothetical Portfolio Simulation

©Own Mountain Trading Company

Figure 2 – Buy-and-Hold Portfolio Allocation Exploration, Hypothetical Portfolio Simulation

(Visit truthaboutetfrotation.com/book-owners/ to download all graphics and trade-by-trade backtesting data)

Commentary on Mutual Fund Portfolio

The array of results lets us compare the effects of adding more bonds to a portfolio. Of course, going forward the numbers won't be the same, but we can still learn from relative comparisons since each experiment in Figure 2 was run on 1998 – 2011.

First off, notice that consistently across the board the maximum drawdown (Max DD %) decreased as more bonds were added to the portfolio. This is graphed in Figure 3. The percentage of stock vs. bonds in the portfolio is marked out along the bottom. The amount of stock in the portfolio decreases as we move left to right in the graph. Since drawdown is a negative number which becomes less negative as more bonds are added to the portfolio, the line goes up and to the right in Figure 3.

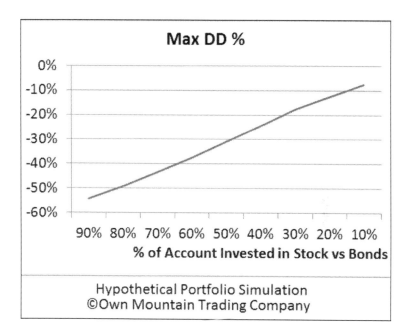

Figure 3 – Maximum Drawdown of Portfolio Exploration

Interestingly enough, the CAGR also increased when going from the extreme of 90% stocks to the balanced situation of 50% stocks / 50% bonds. Adding more bonds than 50% again decreased the CAGR but also decreased the max drawdown. See Figure 4.

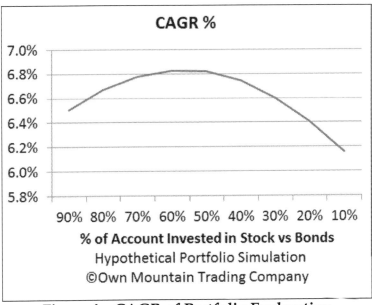

Figure 4 – CAGR of Portfolio Exploration

The average annual returns were consistently decreasing with less stock in the portfolio. This discrepancy with the actual profit (row 3 of Figure 2) is why average annual returns are presented in smaller print than CAGR. The average of all the years together can obscure the order dependency of returns (getting a profit before a loss is better than taking a loss then profit because in the latter case, the profit comes on a smaller account balance). Figure 5 shows graphically how the average annual returns changed with more bonds in the portfolio.

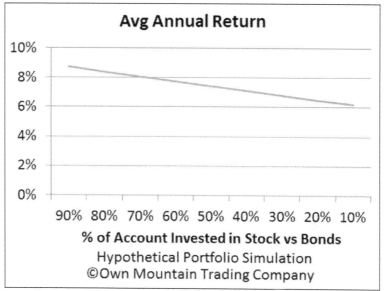

Figure 5 – Average Annual Return of Portfolio Exploration

Volatility went down with more bonds – that was the point. You can see the effect that had on the Sharpe ratio in Figure 6 below, whose annual values only got above 1 for the case of 20% stocks and 80% bonds. Clearly this was a tough time period to hold onto stocks, even with a diversified portfolio.

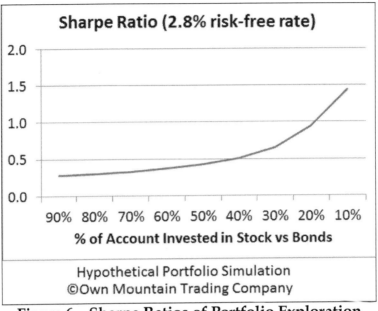

Figure 6 – Sharpe Ratios of Portfolio Exploration

On the monthly statistics, the average return (in Figure 2, row 6) again decreased as the proportion of stocks held in the portfolio decreased. At the same time, the volatility decreased, although the volatility for one month (in Figure 2, row 7) was more than one-twelfth the yearly volatility. The result was that the monthly Sharpe ratios (in Figure 2, row 10) were lower than the annual Sharpe ratios(in Figure 2, row 5).

Comparing monthly Sharpe ratio to Sortino ratio (in Figure 2, row 11), the Sortino ratio was always greater, as expected. The basic trend is the same: as more bonds are added to the portfolio the reward/risk ratio goes up. To say it another way, by adding stocks to the portfolio, one gets more return and even more risk – the risk goes up faster than the return.

This calls to mind a favorite quote: "A ship in a harbour is safe, but that is not what ships are for." - John A. Shedd

Anyway, back to the statistics. The number of trades (in Figure 2, row 12) was never more than the number of funds in the portfolio times the number of years because each position came up for annual rebalancing. With small allocations of high-priced tickers, a position sometimes didn't change in the rebalancing, resulting in fewer than the theoretical maximum number of trades.

If you look at the raw trade lists on the companion web site, you'll see many trades left open at the end of the simulation. That's because each time a few more shares were bought during rebalancing, a new trade was created. This makes it easier to understand what the simulator did and also keeps track of tax lots, which may be useful in the future.

As you'll see later, some other strategies actually traded less frequently but they turned over the whole portfolio rather than just trading a few shares. I'll touch on the tax implications in a moment.

The Average Hold Time is reported in bars or trading days, of which there are roughly 250 per year. The numbers listed in the bottom row of Figure 2 come out to about 7 years, which was far less than the test period. What happened was that the few shares bought during rebalancing were counted as independent trades and brought the average down.

The Win Rate (in Figure 2, row 13) was quite high for all the portfolios – over 90%. The 10/90 and 30/70 even reached 100% wins! Every single asset in the portfolio was up from 1998 to 2011, so where did the losses come from? Rebalancing.

What If You Didn't Rebalance

Since rebalancing is a bit of a hassle, what if we skipped it? I tested that out with the 50/50 stock/bond mix. As you can see from the rightmost column of Figure 7, not rebalancing cost 0.9% in CAGR, when taxes were not considered. The stats in this case were slightly worse for just letting the garden grow wild.

1998 - 2011 with Mutual Funds	Rebalance	No Rebalance
Stock % / Bond %	50 / 50	50 / 50
Individual Stock Fund %	12.5%	12.5%
CAGR %	6.8%	5.9%
Max DD %	-31.0%	-35.8%
Annual Sharpe Ratio (2.8% risk-free rate)	0.42	0.32
Funds: VFINX, NAESX, VEIEX, VGTSX, VBMFX		

Figure 7 – No Rebalancing

Comparison with S&P 500

Okay, so I can't resist a comparison between the diversified portfolios and holding only the S&P 500 for the same time period, 1998 – 2011. As you can see from the right hand column of Figure 2, the S&P 500 produced a 3.6% CAGR, a -55% drawdown, and an annual Sharpe ratio of only 0.14. The returns are smaller, the drawdown deeper, the reward/risk ratios lower.

Clearly putting everything on the S&P 500 was not a big win. We have got to find ways to do better! It appeared that simply holding / rebalancing a diversified portfolio which includes other funds along with the S&P 500 is one possible strategy. We will look at active strategies, such as ETF Rotation, as well.

Report and Commentary on ETF Portfolio from 2005 - 2011

Figure 8 shows the simulated results of applying the exact same diversified portfolio strategies to the ETFs (SPY, IWM, EFA, EEM, AGG) over the period 2005 – 2011. In general, the same relationships hold as for the longer time period with mutual funds so I won't go through it in detail.

Stock % / Bond %	90 / 10	80 / 20	70 / 30	60 / 40	50 / 50	40 / 60	30 / 70	20 / 80	10 / 90	SP500
Individual Stock Fund %	22.5%	20%	17.5%	15%	12.5%	10%	7.5%	5%	2.5%	SPY
CAGR %	5.0%	5.3%	5.6%	5.8%	5.8%	5.8%	5.8%	5.7%	5.5%	2.6%
Max DD %	-53.6%	-48.4%	-42.4%	-36.6%	-30.4%	-23.6%	-20.2%	-17.0%	-14.4%	-55.1%
Annual Sharpe Ratio (2.8% risk-free rate)	0.22	0.24	0.26	0.29	0.34	0.41	0.54	0.89	1.83	0.10

2005 - 2011 Buy and Hold Portfolio Simulation with Exchange Traded Funds (ETFs)

Funds: SPY, IWM, EEM, EFA, AGG

©Own Mountain Trading Company

Hypothetical Portfolio Simulation

Figure 8 – ETF Portfolio Buy-and-Hold

For 2005 – 2011, the asset allocation that produced the most returns with the least drawdown was 40% stocks and 60% bonds with 5.8% CAGR and -23% drawdown. The 30 / 70 portfolio did what looks like the same CAGR with a drawdown of only -20%. Double-clicking into the trade-by-trade results spreadsheet shows that 40 / 60 did just a smidge better.

Mixing in even more bonds reduced the drawdown further but clearly at the expense of the CAGR. Going to the other extreme with 90% stocks and 10% bonds brought the win rate down to 83% with commensurate damage to the CAGR and maximum drawdown.

Tax Implications of Portfolio Adjustments

(The following tax assumptions might not apply to you, check with your tax advisor.)

In discussing the number of trades, we noted that rebalancing the portfolio every year required up to one trade per ticker. But those trades were often only a small percentage of the account – not a complete turnover of assets. For taxable accounts (not IRA or 401k), you might assume the tax due to rebalancing would be negligible.

In fact, I made an estimate of paying 15% tax - the current long-term capital gains rate for holdings over a year which assumes rebalancing at least 366 days apart. The tax impact of rebalancing on our example was 0.01% CAGR – nothing to get excited about.

Gross-Up for After-Tax Comparisons

One of the advantages of this gentle diversified portfolio might still be taxes. To make better comparisons with more active strategies, we can estimate the return required from an active strategy before taxes to match the buy-and-hold strategy with a no-tax assumption.

In reality, you may still owe taxes just for holding a mutual fund because any capital gains taken by the mutual fund will flow through to you. Even index funds make adjustments such as rebalancing or tracking companies that come and go from the index. This may result in taxes even in a buy-and-hold situation – check with your tax advisor.

The top line of Figure 9 shows the return in the ideal case of no taxes. Each row corresponds to a tax rate: 10%, 15%, 25%, 28%, 33%, 35%. The intersection of the row and columns estimates what the taxable return would have to be to net out to the top line return.

Tax Rate	Gross-Up of Tax-Free Return				
0%	6.8%	3%	5%	5.8%	10%
10%	7.6%	3.3%	5.6%	6.4%	11.1%
15%	8.0%	3.5%	5.9%	6.8%	11.8%
25%	9.1%	4.0%	6.7%	7.7%	13.3%
28%	9.4%	4.2%	6.9%	8.1%	13.9%
33%	10.1%	4.5%	7.5%	8.7%	14.9%
35%	10.5%	4.6%	7.7%	8.9%	15.4%

Figure 9 – Tax Gross-Up

For example, if the tax-free portfolio showed returns of 6.8%, then a fully taxable strategy that turns over its whole portfolio within a year would have to show a return of 9.1% to be equivalent for an investor in a 25% tax bracket.

The Reference Portfolio or Baseline for Comparison

The goal of this chapter was to create a reference portfolio we can use as a baseline for comparison to more active strategies. Making several backtesting runs added informative insight.

Now it's time to pick a single portfolio to be our reference for comparison. I focused in on the 50/50 mix because it did the best for the longest timeframe. The actual mix of assets is shown in Figure 10.

Asset	Allocation	Mutual Fund	ETF
US Large Cap Stocks	12.5%	VFINX	SPY or IVV
US Small Cap Stocks	12.5%	NAESX	IWM
Int'l Developed Markets	12.5%	VGTSX	EFA
Int'l Emerging Markets	12.5%	VEIEX	EEM
US Bonds	50%	VBMFX	AGG

Figure 10 – Reference Portfolio Asset Allocation

Backtesting results are summarized in Figure 11 below. Figure 12 shows the year-by-year return of the reference portfolio as well.

Simulated Backtesting Performance of Diversified Reference Portfolio	1998-2011 Mutual Funds	2005 - 2011 ETFs
Funds	VFINX, NAESX, VEIEX, VGTSX, VBMFX	SPY, IWM, EEM, EFA, AGG
Stock % / Bond %	50 / 50	50 / 50
Individual Stock Fund %	12.5%	12.5%
CAGR %	6.8%	5.8%
Max DD %	-31.0%	-30.4%
Annual Sharpe Ratio (2.8% risk-free rate)	0.42	0.34

Hypothetical Portfolio Simulation

©Own Mountain Trading Company

Figure 11 – Reference Portfolio Performance Summary

Total Returns	Buy and Hold + Rebalancing	
	Mutual Fund	ETF Portfolio
Funds	VFINX, NAESX, VEIEX, VGTSX, VBMFX	SPY, IWM, EEM, EFA, AGG
1998	6.83%	
1999	16.35%	
2000	-0.98%	
2001	0.35%	
2002	-3.63%	
2003	23.07%	
2004	11.92%	
2005	8.64%	8.48%
2006	12.96%	13.13%
2007	11.03%	8.99%
2008	-18.59%	-16.21%
2009	23.81%	19.14%
2010	12.30%	11.51%
2011	-0.37%	-0.26%

Hypothetical Portfolio Simulation
®Own Mountain Trading Company

Figure 12 – Year-by-Year Return of Reference Portfolio

With this diversified reference portfolio, we can now move forward and make meaningful comparisons to more active investment strategies.

What Could Be Better Than Diversified Buy-and-Hold

Just sticking with the diversified portfolio would be great – if it produced more gain with less drawdown!

One common-sense approach to improving performance is to try to shift capital into the top performing assets, riding the gains while staying away from the asset classes which are languishing. To make this work, it needs to do two things:

1. Choose asset classes early enough in their run that they still have room to go up.
2. Don't be so quick to shift asset classes that the portfolio churns, losing with every whipsaw.

The upcoming chapters show you how to do this rotation and how it would have performed historically. Starting with the assets in the diversified portfolio from last section, it builds from basic rotation to more sophisticated techniques using stop losses, plus additional asset classes like short funds, cash, long bonds, and commodities.

How to Do an ETF Rotation

Rules for rotation are necessary to make this experiment – and actual trading – objective and repeatable. Early rotation strategies, especially among sectors of the stock market, attempted to track the current status of the economic and business cycles and shift into areas that should experience growth during the current phase. This is extremely difficult to forecast, even among economic experts. For example, economists don't officially declare a recession until months after it has begun. By then, the stock market has long since priced it in. Also, it is difficult to backtest such judgment calls.

A simpler, more objective approach is to measure the funds' performance at regular intervals and get into those that rank highest. As mentioned above, even though we want to always be in the best funds, it is necessary to give them a little breathing room, by allowing a top fund to place anywhere in the top half before replacing it with a stronger candidate.

The Rate of Change (RoC), which is simply the total return in percentage form, is my preferred metric to select funds because it is easy to understand, quick to calculate, objective, and directly related to performance. A key question, which is answered in the next section, is: how far back does one go to calculate the percentage gain for rotation?

Basic Rotation Rules

Before we get to the test results, let's go through the rotation process in detail. The rotation rules I currently prefer, which were used for this report unless stated otherwise are:
  1. Each week, calculate the percentage total return (including dividends) for each fund.

2. Rank the funds and note
   a. The top two
   b. The cut-off for the top half
3. If the account is 100% cash, split the account 50/50 between the top two funds.
4. If a currently held ETF is in the top half, hold it.
5. If a currently held ETF is not in the top half, then sell it.
6. With significant money available to invest (usually from the sale in step 5), buy the highest performing fund not already owned. The new purchase should be one of the top two ETFs from step 2a. That is,
   a. If not already in the top ETF, buy it.
   b. If already in the top ETF, buy the #2 ETF on the list
   c. If 100% cash, split 50/50 to buy into the top 2 funds.
   d. Re-balance annually to 50/50 split of the top 2 funds.

This method stays invested in the top 2 performers, allowing them to breathe by only selling a fund if it falls into the bottom half of the list. When a fund drops to the bottom half, a replacement is picked from the top of the list. It never doubles into an existing fund but is always invested in two different funds.

For backtesting, the price data is dividend-adjusted in such a way that it appears that dividends were automatically re-invested on the dividend day at the current price with no commission. That's not entirely realistic. First off, not all brokers will allow a commission-free dividend reinvestment. Secondly, it's possible to hold an ETF through the dividend recording date, but rotate out before the dividend is paid, resulting in a cash balance in the account. Personally, I just hold dividends in cash until the next rotation opportunity.

Performance of Rotation of Reference Portfolio

One of the key questions from the previous section was how far to look back to calculate the percentage gain in order to decide which funds to pick. Fortunately, computers are fast workers and we can quickly check several reasonable settings.

The results of rotating among the mutual funds used for the reference portfolio from 1998 – 2011 are shown in Figure 13. Keep in mind this is a hypothetical simulation – the mutual fund company would never let you rotate in and out of the funds like this. We are using mutual funds in the backtest because their history goes back beyond 1998.

The top section in Figure 13 plots the Compound Annual Growth Rates (CAGR) for the rotation strategy in dark gray and buy-and-hold of the diversified reference portfolio in black. The lookback settings go from 20 to 300 trading days, increasing in increments of 10.

At a glance, you can see that all settings of the rotation produced higher returns than holding the reference portfolio. Both the rotation and the reference portfolio have the same assets. The difference is in rotating according to simple rules which historically produced better CAGR.

The bottom of Figure 13 shows a different story. This is the drawdown, expressed as negative numbers. In every case but one, this simple rotation strategy (plotted as the light gray line) demonstrated more volatility as measured by a deeper drawdown than the reference portfolio (plotted as the solid black line).

The dotted black line is the drawdown of the S&P 500, tracked by VFINX. In every case, the rotation strategy was superior to passively holding the large-cap index fund.

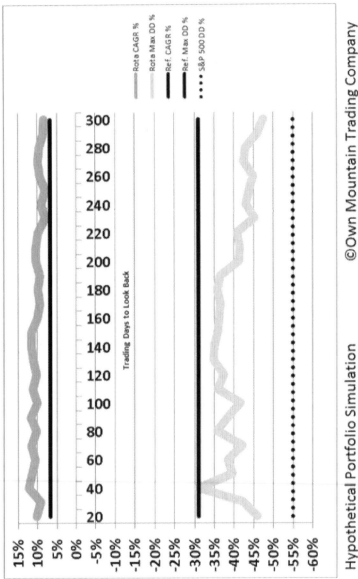

Figure 13 – Rotation Lookback Settings

In practice, we need to select just one setting for the lookback period. We need that for live trading, and to make the rest of the book manageable. To guard against over-optimization, pick a setting that is among a plateau of good settings rather than an isolated peak.

Choosing 140 trading days (between six and seven calendar months) as the lookback period to calculate the percentage gain appears to meet that criterion. Many charting packages will calculate this as a 140-bar RoC – the difficulty is in getting them to operate on total return data. You can download an open source spreadsheet that makes this calculation from my site at truthaboutetfrotation.com.

140-day RoC Rotation Results

A detailed comparison to the reference portfolio of the 140-day rotation for mutual funds and for ETFs is shown in Figure 14. As above, the CAGR is better but the drawdown is worse for rotation. The Sharpe ratio is a single metric that balances both the risk and reward. In Figure 14 you can see that the rotation strategies produced a better Sharpe ratio than buy-and-hold.

	1998 - 2011 with Mutual Funds		2005 - 2011 with ETFs	
	Reference	Rotation	Reference	Rotation
Settings	**50 / 50**	**140 period**	**50 / 50**	**140 period**
Net Profit on $10k init bal	$ 15,191	$ 36,244	$ 4,850	$ 8,607
Overall Profit %	152%	362%	49%	86%
CAGR %	**6.8%**	**11.6%**	**5.8%**	**9.3%**
Max DD %	**-31.0%**	**-35.0%**	**-30.4%**	**-34.4%**
Rough: Profit % / Max DD %	4.9	10.4	1.6	2.5
Max DD Date	9-Mar-09	9-Mar-09	9-Mar-09	9-Mar-09
Avg Annual Return	7.4%	13.3%	6.4%	10.3%
Annual Standard Deviation	10.9%	19.9%	10.7%	14.3%
Annual Sharpe Ratio (2.8% risk-free rate)	0.42	0.53	**0.34**	0.52
Avg Monthly Return	0.59%	1.02%	0.51%	0.85%
Monthly Standard Deviation	2.7%	4.5%	2.9%	4.6%
Avg Excess Monthly Return over 3-month Treasury Rate	0.37%	0.79%	0.34%	0.68%
Monthly Excess Standard Deviati	2.7%	4.5%	2.9%	4.5%
Monthly Excess Sharpe Ratio	0.13	0.18	0.12	0.15
Monthly Excess Sortino Ratio	0.22	0.32	0.19	0.27
Total Trades	63	173	28	93
Win Rate	97%	57%	96%	63%
Lose Rate	3%	40%	4%	37%
Avg Win %	87%	10%	42%	8%
Avg Loss %	-10%	-4%	-13%	-4%
Avg Bars Held	757	59	1004	56
Hypothetical Portfolio Simulation	©Own Mountain Trading Company			

Figure 14 – Simulated Rotation Performance

(Visit truthaboutetfrotation.com/book-owners/ to download all graphics and trade-by-trade backtesting data)

The number of trades for the rotation strategy was roughly three times that of buy-and-hold. The win rate dropped considerably, and the size of the wins decreased as well. The rotation strategy lost a greater percentage of the time. Overall, however, the rotation strategy accumulated more gains, as evidenced by the higher CAGR.

The average number of bars held at the bottom of Figure 14 shows that the rotation strategies stuck with one fund for an average of less than 60 trading days. This is about 12 weeks or one calendar quarter. We can expect the full portfolio to turn over within a year and so should assume all gains would be taxed at the short term rate, if held in a taxable account.

If held in an IRA and traded with limit orders at a broker that offers a commission-free arrangement, the turnover doesn't necessarily add to overhead.

Tax Considerations

One of the oft-cited benefits of buy-and-hold is tax considerations. Referring back to the "gross-up" table in Figure 10, to come out ahead a mutual fund rotation strategy would need to produce gains of 9.1% for a middle (25%) tax bracket and 10.5% for the top federal (36%) tax bracket. The 140-day rotation came in at 11.6% to stay ahead after taxes.

For the ETF portfolios over 2005 – 2011, buy-and-hold produced 5.8% CAGR and rotation got 9.3% CAGR before taxes. 5.8% grosses up to 8.8% at a high federal tax rate so the rotation just squeaked by, and in fact may not be viable for a taxpayer in the top bracket with state tax to contend with besides.

For most tax brackets, however, I think this shows that running a rotation strategy in an after-tax account is not out of the question. Of course, your personal situation may be different, consult your tax advisor.

Year-by-Year Returns

Year-by-year total returns are reported in Figure 15. Comparing back to Figure 12 for the reference portfolio gives insight into how rotation produced higher gains with greater volatility.

Total Returns 140-day Rotation	Mutual Fund VFINX, NAESX, VEIEX, VGTSX, VBMFX	ETF Portfolio SPY, IWM, EEM, EFA, AGG
1998	11.5%	
1999	37.1%	
2000	-12.2%	
2001	4.9%	
2002	-10.5%	
2003	50.6%	
2004	8.5%	
2005	20.2%	19.5%
2006	21.7%	18.7%
2007	22.1%	18.7%
2008	-18.2%	-16.6%
2009	42.6%	28.4%
2010	8.7%	4.0%
2011	-0.9%	-0.7%

Hypothetical Portfolio Simulation
©Own Mountain Trading Compan¡

Figure 15 – Year-by-Year Performance of Basic Rotation Strategy

In two of the four down years, the rotation did considerably worse. In 2000, the buy-and-hold portfolio only gave up 1% overall while the rotation lost 12%. Again in 2002, buy-and-hold gave up 3.6% compared to 10.5% loss for rotation. Neither did well in 2008, with comparable losses of 18% for mutual funds and 16% for ETFs. Finally, in 2011 both methods showed small losses.

In the profitable years rotation made up for any losses. Only in 2004 and 2010 did sitting on the diversified portfolio make more money than the rotation. Rotating the mutual funds often showed more than twice the gains, however, the strategy is too active to carry out on mutual funds. With the ETFs, the superiority is less pronounced but still very evident. In 2005 - 2007, the rotation blasted out roughly 19% per year while buy-and-hold spent two of those years with single digit gains.

2009 produced curious results: 42% versus 24% with mutual funds, 29% versus 19% with ETFs for rotation versus buy-and-hold respectively. First of all, why the differences between mutual funds and ETFs? Largely it is because the funds do not always track the same indices with the same representative instruments, even though they may follow the same asset class. Also, they have different fee structures but that is a smaller impact.

Checking the trade-by-trade data for 2009 illustrates the differences. Between buying shares in 3/26/09 and selling a few shares to rebalance on 01/04/10, VEIEX gained 70% while EEM was only up 64%. The majority of the emerging market shares bought on 3/26/09 were sold on 2/25/10 for a gain of 56% for VEIEX or on 2/10/10 for a gain of 50% on EEM. In just this one trade, there was a 6% difference in performance between VEIEX and EEM!

This example also illustrates the value of rebalancing because roughly 15% in profits dissipated between the annual rebalancing exit and the rotation to another fund. Experiments with more frequent rebalancing are reported in a later chapter.

Overall, the backtesting tended to validate the rotation strategy over buy-and-hold for all but the most tax-sensitive traders.

What If You Don't Own a Home?

Investors who don't own a home, or who want more exposure to the real estate asset class, may be curious to see what happens with the rotation strategy when a real estate fund is added.

To produce Figure 16, the same rules were applied to the same funds as Figure 13, except that FRESX was added to the mix. FRESX is a Fidelity mutual fund that focuses on real estate companies, both domestic to the United States and international. It was chosen because it is one of the few pure real estate funds dating back to the 1990s. In recent years, FRESX performance was generally higher than IYR, an ETF that tracks a real estate index.

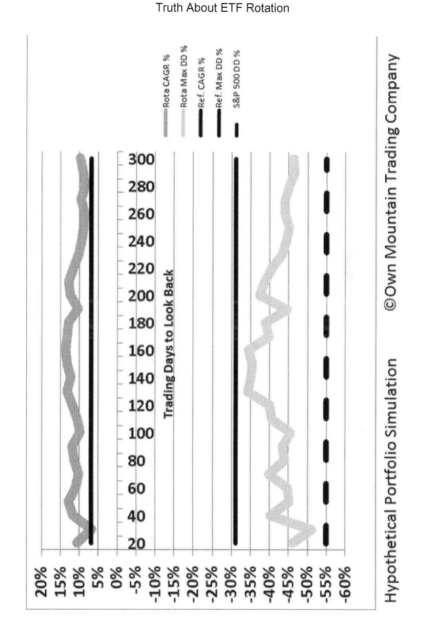

Figure 16 – Rotation Performance by Lookback Period with Real Estate

As before, the dark gray line in Figure 16 shows the CAGR of the rotation strategy for various settings. The light gray line plots the drawdown. Compare to the solid black lines for the performance of the reference portfolio. The dashed line is the S&P 500 drawdown.

The general results are about the same with real estate as without: the rotation strategy produced higher returns but with worse drawdown. With real estate, it appears that the sweet spot for the lookback period grows to 160 days.

Which Day of the Week to Rotate?

Most of the runs for this book rotated the ETFs on Thursday, using the closing price on Thursday. What happened if a different day of the week was adopted? Not much difference, according to Figure 17.

Wednesday came out on top with a 13.9% CAGR. Monday was the laggard at 12.6% CAGR, confirming its reputation as a hard day. Thursday placed second with 13.7% CAGR.

No surprises in these results. That they were clustered together suggests this is a robust strategy. A wide variation would be a red flag. However, it is extremely unlikely that all days of the week would produce exactly the same statistics. One of the days has to come out on top and it happened to be Wednesday in this experiment.

I don't know of a good reason why Wednesday should stay on top, yet after seeing Figure 17, I'm making my rotation trades based on the closing price on Wednesday.

Since the closing prices and ranking are not necessarily known in time to place a real trade, I enter limit orders to execute on Thursday, pegged to the closing prices on Wednesday. This also serves to contain slippage. If my limit order is not filled by the end of the day Thursday, I will change it to a market order to be sure the trade happens.

1998 - 2011 with Mutual Funds	Reference	Rotation	Rotation	Rotation	Rotation	Rotation
	no FRESX	Funds: VFINX, NAESX, VEIEX, VGTSX, VBMFX, FRESX				
Settings	**50 / 50**	**160,Mon**	**160,Tues**	**160,Wed**	**160,Thur**	**160,Fri**
CAGR %	6.8%	12.6%	12.8%	13.9%	13.7%	13.2%
Max DD %	-31.0%	-35.7%	-34.4%	-34.4%	-34.4%	-34.2%
Annual Sharpe Ratio (2.8% risk-free rate)	0.42	0.63	0.65	0.66	0.65	0.63

Hypothetical Portfolio Simulation

©Own Mountain Trading Company

Figure 17 – Day of the Week Comparison

Bring on the Long Bonds

Our basic list of ETFs to rotate consists of four stock funds and one bond fund. With this mix, it is never possible to get entirely out of the stock market during a downdraft.

Adding another bond fund changes that by giving two safe havens from the stock market. We'll later look at rotating to cash. For now, funds that track the long US Treasury bonds will serve. To implement this from the historical perspective the VUSTX mutual fund from Vanguard was included in the backtest. For more recent perspective and live trading the ETF from iShares, TLT, is the choice.

Figure 18 shows the results of applying the same rotation rules to the mutual funds (VFINX, NAESX, VEIEX, VGTSX, VBMFX, VUSTX) during 1998 – 2011. Then the ETFs (SPY, IWM, EEM, EFA, AGG, TLT) were backtested during 2005 – 2011. One more time period, 2009 – 2011, was added in order to see how the strategy worked lately.

In head-to-head comparison, we can see that including the long bond funds, VUSTX or TLT, added value early on by boosting CAGR from 11.6% to 13.5% and reducing drawdowns from -35% to -20.9% for the mutual funds during 1998 – 2011. Even more impressive: with the ETFs from 2005 – 2011 the CAGR jumped from 9.3% to 15.8% while the drawdown dropped from -34% to -21%.

From 2009 – 2011, when the stock market largely went up, occasionally rotating into TLT slightly increased CAGR from 9.7% to 10.1% and allowed a max drawdown of -15.1% compared to -16%.

| | 1998 - 2011 with Mutual Funds | | 2005 - 2011 with ETFs | | 2009 - 2011 with ETFs | |
	Rotation	Rotation	Rotation	Rotation	Rotation	Rotation
Settings	140 basic	140 add VUSTX	140 basic	140 add TLT	140 basic	140 add TLT
CAGR %	11.6%	13.5%	9.3%	15.8%	9.7%	10.1%
Max DD %	-35.0%	-20.9%	-34.4%	-21.1%	-16.0%	-15.1%
Annual Sharpe Ratio (2.8% risk-free rate)	0.53	0.81	0.52	1.73	0.60	0.92

Hypothetical Portfolio Simulation   ©Own Mountain Trading Company

Figure 18 – Rotation with Long Bonds

Shorting the Market with Inverse Funds

The next set of comparisons takes place between 2007 and 2011 because that's when index fund ETFs became available to track commodities and short funds. (Yes, inverse mutual funds were available sooner but the overhead of tracking many different time periods was getting too much.) The second and third columns of Figure 19 are reruns in the 2007 – 2011 time period to give points for comparison.

As you can see comparing the second and third columns of Figure 19 it's a toss-up between TLT and inverse fund SH as a fifth wheel in the rotation strategy. TLT in column 3 produced a 13.2% CAGR with almost -15% max drawdown.

SH moved a couple percentage points in the wrong direction with 11.2% CAGR and -17.7% max drawdown. Including both SH and TLT brought the CAGR up slightly to 14.2% with a slight worsening of max drawdown to -16.8%. Note that the basic ETF rotation performance came in at 5.4% CAGR with -34% drawdown during this very tough time period.

Adding both TLT and SH improved the situation during the 2008 credit crisis.

2007 - 2011 with ETFs	Rotation	Rotation	Rotation	Rotation	Rotation	Rotation
Settings	140 ETFs	140+TLT	140+SH	140+TLT+SH	140+DBC	140+All
CAGR %	5.4%	13.2%	11.2%	14.2%	9.1%	15.5%
Max DD %	-34.2%	-15.1%	-17.7%	-16.8%	-41.3%	-21.8%
Annual Sharpe Ratio (2.8% risk-free rate)	0.25	1.40	0.84	1.40	0.43	1.41

Hypothetical Portfolio Simulation

©Own Mountain Trading Company

Figure 19 – Including an Inverse Fund to Short the Market

How About Those Commodities?

Commodities have the potential for gain. Unfortunately, they bring volatility with them. Column 6 in Figure 19, above, shows that adding commodity index fund DBC to the basic ETF mix during 2007 – 2011 improved CAGR to 9% -- above the basic ETFs but below SH and/or TLT. The max drawdown hit new lows at -41% though.

Everything But the Kitchen Sink

Bringing a full complement of ETFs - SPY, IWM, EEM, EFA, AGG, TLT, SH, DBC – boosted the CAGR to 15.5% while widening the max drawdown to -21.8%. See the rightmost column in Figure 19. Clearly, tinkering with the list of ETFs produced gains at the expense of increases in volatility.

Comparing back to buy-and-hold of a diversified portfolio continued to show the benefits of rotation. In this case, Figure 20 shows backtests for 2007 – 2011 where the reference portfolio of 50% stock index funds and 50% AGG bond fund brought in only 3.8% CAGR with a whopping -30% max drawdown.

Splitting the bond allocation between AGG's broad spectrum and TLT's focus on 20-year treasuries helped somewhat by creating a CAGR of 5.8% with a -27% drawdown. Making room for commodities was not worth the effort as the CAGR came in at 4% with a -38% max drawdown.

2007 - 2011 with ETFs	Rebalance	Rebalance	Rebalance
Settings for ETFS: AGG, EEM, EFA, IWM, SPY	50% stocks, 50% AGG	50% Stocks, 25%AGG, 25%TLT	ETFS + TLT + DBC (Equal Shares)
CAGR %	3.8%	5.8%	4.0%
Max DD %	-30.2%	-26.7%	-38.3%
Annual Sharpe Ratio (2.8% risk-free rate)	0.14	0.40	0.16

Hypothetical Portfolio Simulation   ©Own Mountain Trading Company

Figure 20 – Buy-and-Hold Reference Portfolio 2007-2011

Rotating to Cash when Everything Rots

The previous sections demonstrated the benefits of being able to completely take money out of the stock market on occasion. Allocating assets to bond funds or even short funds both increased the returns and decreased the maximum drawdown.

However, bond funds, especially long bonds such as 20-year treasury bonds in TLT, can be volatile themselves. The price of a long-term bond is sensitive to interest rates and other factors. It is not risk free. "Risk-free Treasuries" refers to short-term Treasury Bills which do not fluctuate much during their brief lifespan.

Inverse funds are not only volatile; they come with higher built-in expenses. Worse, an inverse fund is not designed to track the market for long periods; they only try to offset the daily behavior of the underlying index.

What if we simply hold assets in cash when the funds are not performing well? When the percentage gain over the last 140 trading days falls below zero, it says the fund has lost money on an intermediate-term basis. We can take that as a signal to move to cash.

The revised rules for rotation, including a safe haven in cash, are:
1. Each week, calculate the percentage total return (including dividends) for each fund.
2. Rank the funds and note
   a. The top two
   b. The cut-off for the top half
   c. Which funds have positive gains over the past 140-days
3. If the account is 100% cash, split the account 50/50 between the top two funds which have positive

performance over the past 140-days. If no funds have positive performance, just stay in cash.

4. If a currently held ETF is in the top half with positive gains, hold it.
5. If a currently held ETF is not in the top half, or is not showing positive gains, then sell it.
6. With money available to invest (usually from the sale in step 5), buy the highest performing fund not already owned with positive gains. The new purchase should be one of the top two ETFs from step 2a. That is:
   a. If not already in the top ETF and the top ETF had positive gains, buy it.
   b. If already in the top ETF, buy the #2 ETF on the list, if it had positive gains.
   c. If 100% cash, split 50/50 to buy into the top 2 funds with positive gains.
   d. Re-balance annually to 50/50 split of the top 2 funds with positive gains.

Doing the full-scale backtest resulted in the statistics in Figure 21. The second and third columns show the results of rotating among mutual funds and cash for the period 1998 – 2011.

Relying on only the basic funds (VFINX, NAESX, VEIEX, VGTSX, VBMFX) with cash added did better but with higher drawdown than including long bonds via VUSTX.

To see where using cash as an asset improved the results, compare the basic+cash run with CAGR of 11% and max drawdown of -28% with the original rotation in Figure 14 which produced a similar CAGR of 11% but worse drawdown of -35%.

However, Figure 18 showed 13.5% CAGR and -20.9% max drawdown for rotation among basic mutual funds and the long bond fund VUSTX. That turned out to be a better performance than including both cash and long bonds as shown in Figure 21, column 2.

Using ETFs for the period 2005 – 2011 again showed that adding cash to the menu of choices reduced the max drawdown from -34% to -22.8% and at the same time the CAGR crept up from 9.3%. to 10.8%. However, from Figure 18 we saw that rotation among the Basic ETFs + TLT produced a CAGR of 15.8% with -21% drawdown.

During 2007 – 2011 the results with and without cash are about the same, suggesting that some of the funds always gained during that time. This period included the 2008 credit crisis in which TLT soared while the stock market crashed.

So we must conclude that rotating to cash did not always get the best or safest performance. Selecting the right mix of funds produced better results. In a later chapter which double-checks the asset mix over a longer time period, the benefits of cash rotation were even less clear. Cash rotation also brings additional steps in a slightly more complicated set of rules for rotation.

However, cash rotation limited the drawdowns without making a negative impact on returns with the basic set of funds. It is worthwhile to include cash as an asset class in the rotation because we have no guarantee that the same funds will outperform in the future. In the next crash, it may not be TLT that represents safe haven and then cash might be a welcome respite from the markets.

Cash as Asset in Rotation: Only Pick Funds with Positive Gains Over the Last 140 Trading Days

Settings	1998 - 2011 Basic Funds +Cash	1998 - 2011 Funds+VUSTX +Cash	2005 - 2011 Basic ETFs +Cash	2005 - 2011 ETFs+TLT+ Cash	2007 - 2011 ETFs+TLT +SH+Cash	2007 - 2011 All ETFs+Cash
CAGR %	11.1%	11.3%	10.8%	13.4%	13.9%	18.4%
Max DD %	-28.4%	-23.3%	-21.8%	-21.1%	-16.7%	-17.9%
Annual Sharpe Ratio (2.8% risk-free rate)	0.50	0.61	0.68	1.26	1.40	1.92

©Own Mountain Trading Company

Hypothetical Portfolio Simulation

Figure 21 – Cash as an Asset in Rotation

What Happened with Stop Losses

Attempting to shave the drawdowns with stop losses was not very effective. See Figure 22 for data. All runs used the basic set of mutual funds with cash as an asset class, over the timeframe 1998 – 2011. The stop loss was set at a fixed percentage below the entry price and triggered a sale if the stop price was hit while the fund was held.

In general, the performance suffered. The CAGR went down and yet the drawdown got worse. This illustrated the effects of thrashing between funds as they take short-term pullbacks. At 10% and even 15% stop losses the gains were pinched without any improvement in the drawdown.

Stop losses of 20% and 25% produced exactly the same results as the unconstrained runs with cash as an asset class. This means the stops were never hit when placed 20% below the buy price.

Rotating weekly is designed to give each asset enough room to breathe yet cut off losers before they plummet too far. It appears that works better than setting stop losses – at least when cash was considered one of the asset classes.

When cash was not one of the asset classes, stop losses served to reduce the drawdown as illustrated in Figure 23. Stopping out after a loss of 10% from the entry price and then picking another fund squeezed out slightly better CAGR and drawdown compared with cash rotation.

However, stop losses in particular get idealized treatment in historical simulations. My brokers have advised me that my real stop loss orders in the market may not be honored if the market drops quickly. If they are filled, it may be at a much lower price as the market could plunge mid-day but recover by the close. In summary, going to cash may be easier and safer than counting on a stop loss to avert disaster.

Basic Mutual Funds, Basic Rotation 1998 - 2011	No stops	5% stop	10% stop	15% stop	20% stop	25% stop
CAGR %	11.6%	10.1%	12.1%	11.1%	12.4%	11.7%
Max DD %	-35.0%	-30.4%	-27.1%	-33.1%	-28.5%	-32.3%
Annual Sharpe Ratio (2.8% risk-free rate)	0.53	0.46	0.57	0.50	0.57	0.55

Hypothetical Portfolio Simulation   ©Own Mountain Trading Company

Figure 22 – Rotation with Stop Losses and Cash as an Asset

Basic Mutual Funds, Basic Rotation 1998 - 2011	No stops	5% stop	10% stop	15% stop	20% stop	25% stop
CAGR %	11.6%	10.1%	12.1%	11.1%	12.4%	11.7%
Max DD %	-35.0%	-30.4%	-27.1%	-33.1%	-28.5%	-32.3%
Annual Sharpe Ratio (2.8% risk-free rate)	0.53	0.46	0.57	0.50	0.57	0.55

Hypothetical Portfolio Simulation   ©Own Mountain Trading Company

Figure 23 – Stop Losses without Cash as an Asset

Does Active Rebalancing Help Grab Profits?

One last attempt to grab more gains involves rebalancing more frequently to try to catch a fund while it is up and rotate a portion of the profits into the next one that might advance. Figure 24 tells us that monthly rebalancing offered no reward for the extra work while weekly rebalancing was counter-productive.

Compare Different Rebalancing Timeframes for Funds + VUSTX + RYURX	1998 - 2011	1998 - 2011	1998 - 2011
Settings	Annual Rebalance	Monthly Rebalance	Weekly Rebalance
CAGR %	13.5%	13.7%	12.7%
Max DD %	-22.1%	-22.3%	-22.5%
Annual Sharpe Ratio (2.8% risk-free rate)	0.75	0.74	0.77

Hypothetical Portfolio Simulation   ©Own Mountain Trading Company

Figure 24 – Rotation with Frequent Rebalancing

Double-Checking the Asset Mix

In later years, the inverse fund SH helped contain the drawdowns and even add profit while the stock market fell. Just to be sure using inverse funds is a good idea – because it is notoriously difficult to make money on the short side of the market – I did one more set of backtesting runs shown in Figure 25.

Again, including Treasuries with VUSTX and an inverse fund, RYURX, squeezed out 2% more CAGR with a little less drawdown. Definitely this mix won during 1998 – 2011.

Curiously, the longer term results with stocks, bonds, long treasuries, inverse funds, and cash as assets came in slightly behind the simpler rotation without cash but all the same funds as assets. Allowing a rotation into cash when the funds are down intuitively feels safer and allows the investor to stand aside if all other asset classes are getting whacked.

Long-Term Rotation with Cash and Inverse Funds	1998 - 2011	1998 - 2011	1998 - 2011	1998 - 2011
Settings	Basic Funds + Cash	Funds + VUSTX + Cash	Funds+VUSTX+ RYURX + Cash	Funds+VUSTX +RYURX, no cash
CAGR %	11.1%	11.3%	13.0%	13.5%
Max DD %	-23.3%	-28.4%	-22.1%	-22.1%
Annual Sharpe Ratio (2.8% risk-free rate)	0.50	0.61	0.73	0.75

Hypothetical Portfolio Simulation   ©Own Mountain Trading Company

Figure 25 – Long-term Backtest with an Inverse Fund

Which Strategies Beat the Crash

Almost every rotation strategy produced more profits than buy-and-hold of the reference portfolio, although sometimes those profits came at the expense of greater drawdowns.

Adding an inverse fund and a 20-year Treasury bond fund did the most to beef up gains while pruning drawdowns. Rotating to cash offered downside protection without much performance hit. Stop losses did not improve on a weekly rotation with cash as an asset. Neither did rebalancing frequently.

To summarize, the ultimate strategy of the bunch tested in this book relied on these funds:

- SPY or IVV for S&P 500 stocks
- IWM for Russell 2000 small-cap stocks
- EEM for Emerging Market stocks
- EFA for International Developed Market stocks
- AGG for Barclay's composite bond index
- TLT for 20-year Treasury bonds
- SH for inverse S&P 500

...traded in a weekly rotation among the top two funds, according to these rules:

1. Each week, calculate the percentage total return (including dividends) for each fund.
2. Rank the funds and note
   a. The top two
   b. The cut-off for the top half
   c. Which funds have positive gains over the past 140-days
3. If the account is 100% cash, split the account 50/50 between the top two funds which have positive

performance over the past 140-days. If no funds have positive performance, just stay in cash.

4. If a currently held ETF is in the top half with positive gains, hold it.

5. If a currently held ETF is not in the top half, or is not showing positive gains, then sell it.

6. With money available to invest (usually from the sale in step 5), buy the highest performing fund not already owned with positive gains. The new purchase should be one of the top two ETFs from step 2a. That is:

   a. If not already in the top ETF and the top ETF had positive gains, buy it.

   b. If already in the top ETF, buy the #2 ETF on the list, if it had positive gains.

   c. If 100% cash, split 50/50 to buy into the top 2 funds with positive gains.

   d. Re-balance annually to 50/50 split of the top 2 funds with positive gains.

...which produced the following results in hypothetical historical simulation:

13% CAGR with -22% maximum drawdown when backtested on mutual funds during 1998 – 2011 and 13.9 % CAGR with -16.7% maximum drawdown when backtested on ETFs during 2007 – 2011. See Figure 26.

Weekly Rotation with 140 Trading Days RoC. No Stops.	1998 - 2011	2007 - 2011
Settings	Funds+VUSTX + RYURX + Cash	ETFs+TLT+SH +Cash
CAGR %	13.0%	13.9%
Max DD %	-22.1%	-16.7%
Annual Sharpe Ratio (2.8% risk-free rate)	0.73	1.40

Hypothetical Portfolio Simulation

©Own Mountain Trading Company

Figure 26 – Hypothetical Performance of the Ultimate ETF Rotation Strategy

Over the longer term, each fund was held, on average, roughly 100 trading days, which is about 5 calendar months. Thus we can assume all trades get taxed at the short term rate. At 13% CAGR, this strategy may still come out ahead for current federal tax brackets compared to buy-and-hold of the reference portfolio.

In a tax-free environment such as an IRA or these backtests, the rotation results were far ahead of buy-and-hold.

Figure 27 shows the year-by-year backtested performance of this ultimate rotation strategy. The detail of buy-and-hold returns for the diversified reference portfolio is repeated right alongside.

The mutual fund backtest results go back to 1998 while the ETF record begins at 2007. Both run to the end of 2011. The differences in results between the mutual funds and ETFs are due to the different fund compositions. Overall, rotation demonstrated substantial gains interspersed with smaller losses and compared favorably to buy-and-hold of a diversified portfolio.

Total Return of Final Rotation Strat			Buy-and-Hold Repeated		
Date	Mutual Funds	ETFs	Mutual Funds	ETFs	
1998	-8.4%		6.8%		
1999	28.0%		16.3%		
2000	-9.2%		-1.0%		
2001	9.9%		0.3%		
2002	4.1%		-3.6%		
2003	49.7%		23.1%		
2004	5.5%		11.9%		
2005	16.2%		8.6%	8.5%	
2006	18.7%		13.0%	13.1%	
2007	20.8%	15.7%	11.0%	9.0%	
2008	14.3%	20.4%	-18.6%	-16.2%	
2009	34.8%	20.0%	23.8%	19.1%	
2010	2.1%	-1.7%	12.3%	11.5%	
2011	10.3%	16.7%	-0.4%	-0.3%	

Hypothetical Portfolio Simulation ©Own Mountain Trading Company

Figure 27 – Ultimate Rotation Strategy Year-by-Year Compared to Holding Reference Portfolio

The equity curves plotted in Figure 28 illustrate how a hypothetical account starting with $10,000 might have fared under rotation (the dark gray line) or buy-and-hold (the black curve).

Rotation won out big-time in the end, but notice that the first five years were a toss-up where buy-and-hold was often ahead.

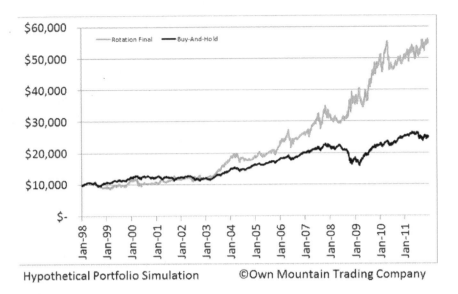

Hypothetical Portfolio Simulation   ©Own Mountain Trading Company

Figure 28 – Equity Curves from Backtesting Ultimate Strategy vs. Buy-and-Hold

In 2006 and 2010, holding the reference portfolio produced less volatility. Keep in mind that the reference portfolio was diversified across several asset classes and makes a strong investment in itself.

From 2004 – 2009, the rotation strategy actually doubled its equity. Zooming in on the credit crisis of 2008, you can see the rotation account growing while the diversified portfolio dropped off dramatically.

Of course, future results will vary. Before investing with any strategy, you should carefully consider your resources and goals as well as the risk of loss.

The next step from here is to forward-test this strategy, which I am doing with live trading in my own retirement account.

You can track progress at on the web at truthaboutetfrotation.com/forward-testing/.

Resources

Web Sites

Visit the special page for owners of this book at
truthaboutetfrotation.com/book-owners/

There you can register to download bonus materials including
- all tables from this book
- an ETF Rotation calculator for Excel
- trade-by-trade backtest data

beathecrash.com – website for this whole series of products

divergence-alerts.com – members can follow along with my ETF rotation strategy and also get a list of the MACD divergences on US stocks, ETFs, and futures

backtestingblog.com – background information on backtesting, including glossary

Videos On Amazon.com
Beat The Crash - Diversified Portfolio Baseline, Vol 1 Disc 1

This educational session lays the foundation for the Beat The Crash series by defining a baseline for comparison of investment strategies. A diversified portfolio is described as well as its hypothetical historical performance. Also covered are metrics for comparing investment strategies.

Beat The Crash - Truth About ETF Rotation, Vol 1 Disc 2
Delves into how to do ETF Rotation and the historical simulated performance of rotating the diversified portfolio introduced in Disc 1.

Software

Rotation Spreadsheet - an open-source spreadsheet that can help you find the top ETFs by calculating the 140-day total percentage gains. It also computes stop losses and attempts to size each trade. Available at truthaboutetfrotation.com.

Related Reading

My current reading list is posted at
http://backtestingblog.com/order/books/

Acknowledgements

Thank you to John Chernicky for his insightful reviews of this book. All errors are mine.

Scott Ajax spotted errors in the original drawdown calculations in my portfolio testing software. I am thankful that he persisted in calling them to my attention until they were fixed. I take responsibility for all remaining bugs and miscalculations.

I am grateful to Aric Egmont at Fidelity Investments for motivating me to give sector rotation a second look, and for publishing my article on the topic.

Thank you to my family and friends for patient understanding and encouragement while I research the market and write.

Hat tip to Pearl Sofaer for publishing her book which inspired me to write mine.

Thank you, Dear Reader, for your attention. The knowledge that you will be reading this book motivated me to put in my best effort.

Kindly consider leaving a REVIEW on Amazon. Thank you!

39210738R00052

Made in the USA
Lexington, KY
11 February 2015